D1476639

IMAGES
of America

SURFING IN
SANTA CRUZ

ON THE COVER: Some members of the original Santa Cruz Surfing Club, established in 1936, sit atop the rails of their boards in the cove at Cowell's Beach. This shot shows the variety of boards members rode in those days. Some still surfed on hollow, 12-foot models, while others rode laminated "planks" that were constructed of solid redwood, balsa, and pine. Rich Thompson (second from left) and Dave "Buster" Steward (fourth from left) are shown here sporting the original club T-shirts. (Photograph by Ed Webber, courtesy Covello and Covello Photography.)

IMAGES
of America

SURFING IN SANTA CRUZ

Thomas Hickenbottom with the
Santa Cruz Surfing Club Preservation Society
and the Santa Cruz Surfing Museum

ARCADIA
PUBLISHING

Copyright © 2009 by Thomas Hickenbottom
with the Santa Cruz Surfing Club Preservation Society and the Santa Cruz Surfing Museum
ISBN 978-0-7385-7076-1

Published by Arcadia Publishing
Charleston, South Carolina

Printed in the United States of America

Library of Congress Control Number: 2009927731

For all general information contact Arcadia Publishing at:
Telephone 843-853-2070
Fax 843-853-0044
E-mail sales@arcadiapublishing.com
For customer service and orders:
Toll-Free 1-888-313-2665

Visit us on the Internet at www.arcadiapublishing.com

*This is dedicated to all Santa Cruzans who embraced the surfing
and beach lifestyle from the earliest of times. This is their story.*

CONTENTS

ACKNOWLEDGMENTS

Many of the photographs that appear in this volume are from the archives of the Santa Cruz Surfing Museum. The author also wishes to thank the many businesses, photographers, surfers, and beach folks who generously shared their photograph collections and remembrances, without whose assistance this book would not have come into fruition: Santa Cruz Seaside Company; O'Neill, Inc.; Covello and Covello Photographers; NHS Industries; Haut Surfboards; Johnny Rice Surfboards; City of Santa Cruz Museum of Natural History; Santa Cruz Public Library; Sam Reid Archives; Bay Photo Labs; Harry Mayo; Dave Singletary; Betty Van Dyke; Ray Stout; Don "Chic" Van Selus; Jim Phillips; Bob Richardson; Larry Daniels; Lloyd Ragon; Al Mitchell; Dave and Kathy Sweet; Rod Lundquist; Peter Cole; Doug Haut; Rich Novak; Jack O'Neill; Pat O'Neill; Don Snyder; Jim Foley; Dennis Bassano; Jerry and Earlene Colfer; Johnny and Rosemari Rice; Danny Anderson; Alan Souza; Gene Hall; Scott Ferguson; Jim Houston; Dave McGuire; Geoff McCormick; Howard "Boots" McGhee; Terry Smith; Rick Stiff; Mike Wilson; Ed James; Fred Nelli; Jon Foster; Kim W. Stoner; Greg and Sue Davidson (administrators of the Fred Hunt Archives); Dan Coyro; Lee "Scorp" Evans; Geoffrey Dunn; Jill James; Tony Arkin; Jeff White; and Dave Kerr.

A special thank-you goes to the surviving members of the Santa Cruz Surfing Club, established in 1936, who shared memories of those early times: Harry Mayo, Bill Grace, Pinky Pedemonte, Lloyd Ragon, Harry Murray, Doug Thorne, Ted Schultz, Pete Muttersbach, Terrence Hickey, and Bob Rittenhouse.

Thank you to all the members of the Santa Cruz Surfing Club Preservation Society for input, guidance, and continuous efforts in supporting the ongoing survival of the Santa Cruz Surfing Museum: Harry Mayo, Pinky Pedemonte, Bill Grace, Doug Thorne, Kim W. Stoner, Jon Foster, Dan Young, Howard "Boots" McGhee, Pat Farley, Pete Ogilvie, Joe Grassi, Matt Micuda, Johnny and Rosemari Rice, Dave Dyc, Pete Noble, and Ward Smith. Thanks to Chris Thompson, of Sound Vision Productions and creator of the documentary *Out of the Blue*, for selfless hours of image scanning; and to Tristan Hickenbottom for technical coaching and use of his Macintosh computer, which handled all image and text files in this collection.

INTRODUCTION

Santa Cruz County lies on the northern tip of Monterey Bay in Central California. Board surfing was first introduced to the United States mainland on July 5, 1885, by three visiting Hawaiian princes who rode waves off Main Beach near where the boardwalk now operates.

Since those early days, the sport of surfing has blossomed into a major cultural and economic force in Santa Cruz and throughout California in general. Home to world-class surfers and epic waves, the Santa Cruz coastline boasts a diverse and dedicated cadre of ocean-loving people.

The evolution of surfing in Santa Cruz is a multifaceted story. This volume represents the first time anyone has combined the early years into one book, and the reader will embark on an in-depth journey through this historic period. The evolution also mirrors the growth of the sport worldwide with a few important exceptions.

Unlike Southern California, with its mild climate, sandy points, and warm water, surfing in Santa Cruz is an entirely different undertaking. Freezing offshore winds, numbing water, strong ocean currents, and a precipitous coastline all add up to an endeavor of deep concentration and dedication. In Santa Cruz, with these chilly waters and challenging conditions, it has been more an exercise in total commitment and bravado. It is not uncommon for the water temperature in the winter to drop under 50 degrees Fahrenheit. The huge north swells that hit the bay in winter often reach heights of more than 20 feet.

Early local surfers braved these challenging conditions without the aid of wet suits, and the rocky coastline could spell death to their boards as well. To swim in those freezing waters in huge surf could even be life threatening to the surfer. A few unfortunate souls found that out the hard way. It was an era for only the boldest and most dedicated of surfers.

This volume of photographs is a testament to those people from the earliest of times who helped define and transform surfing and beach life in Santa Cruz. Hopefully the reader will enjoy this foray into a time when it wasn't crowded in the water and there was great fun and camaraderie on the beaches of Monterey Bay.

This wonderful painting from 2001 by local artist extraordinaire and Pleasure Point Surf Club member Jim Phillips, titled *The Boneyard*, clearly encapsulates surfing in the Santa Cruz area. With challenging surf, cold water, windy conditions, and an ominously rugged coastline, surfing in Santa Cruz offers great thrills for those hardy enthusiasts who choose to enter the waters there. (Courtesy Jim Phillips.)

One

EARLY TIMES

Dorothy Becker was one of the first Santa Cruz residents to surf in Hawai'i. In this 1915 photograph, Becker is standing on the beach at Waikiki next to a redwood plank owned by surfing legend Duke Kahanamoku. Many of the redwood boards that were an integral part of early surfing history in Hawai'i came from slabs of wood milled in the Santa Cruz Mountains. (Courtesy Ed Guzman and the Club Ed Surf School and Camps in Santa Cruz.)

On July 20, 1885, three visiting Hawaiian princes, Jonah Kuhio Kalaniana'ole, David Kawananakoa, and Edward Keli'iahonui, rode waves off Main Beach in Santa Cruz. It was the first time "surfing" was introduced to the U.S. mainland. They had redwood logs cut to slabs from the Grover Lumber Mill in the San Lorenzo Valley, in Santa Cruz. Then the brothers shaped them into surfboards. The boards they made were 15 feet long, weighed 100 pounds, and were carved from first-growth redwood trees. It was more than a decade later that surfing was seen again on local beaches. In the summer of 1896, the weekly edition of the *Santa Cruz Surf* noted, "The boys who go in swimming at Seabright Beach use surfboards to ride the breakers, like the Hawaiians." (Courtesy Jim Phillips.)

11

Santa Cruzan Dorothy Becker rides the waves in perfect trim at Canoes surf break, Waikiki Beach, Oah'u, in the summer of 1915. She sports the traditional one-piece swimsuit and cap of the era. This gives credence to the position that one of the first Santa Cruz residents to surf in Hawai'i was a woman. In those early days, few women took up the sport. (Courtesy Ed Guzman and the Club Ed Surf School and Camps in Santa Cruz.)

Born in 1909, Santa Cruz surfing legend Sam Reid poses in front of Duke Kahanamoku's board on Waikiki Beach in the early 1920s. Reid was a tremendously prolific waterman. He was a lifeguard as well as an avid ocean swimmer. At age 19, he moved to the South Shore of Oah'u and quickly mastered the sport of surfing, befriending the famous Kahanamoku brothers. In 1928 and 1932, he won the surfing championship at Waikiki, which at the time was equivalent to the world championship, competing against the local Hawaiian surfers. (Courtesy Santa Cruz Surfing Museum.)

In 1971, at age 62, Sam Reid made a return visit to Waikiki Beach for a reunion with the Kahanamoku brothers. Here he stands next to a balsa board bearing his name. He rode the board during trips to Hawai'i in the 1950s and stored it in a rack right on the beach. Reid spoke Hawaiian and was highly regarded by the locals. He also set the half-mile surfboard paddling record, which stood from 1931 to 1955. He came back to Santa Cruz in 1950, saying its surf was "equivalent to places in Hawai'i," and declared the area from Cowell's Beach to Steamer Lane as "the perfect surfing spot." He established the 1,000-yard swim championship in Santa Cruz, which later became known as the Santa Cruz Lifeguard Championship. He was the first person to ride waves at the famous Malibu Beach and only one of six people surfing on the West Coast when he started at age 17 in 1926. (Courtesy author's collection.)

Pictured from left to right in the summer of 1941, Santa Cruz Surfing Club (SCSC) members Harry Murray, Harry Mayo, Don "Bosco" Patterson, and Norn Handley lug their hollow boards from the "barn" to the beach at Cowell's for a warm and glassy session with no one else in the surf. It was an era of great friendship and respect in the waves. (Photograph by Ed Webber, courtesy Covello and Covello Photography.)

Eugene "Jeep" Allen (left) and Fred Hunt (right) head into the barn to retrieve their boards for a surf session at Cowell's Beach. The barn was located a block north of Cowell's on Bay Street. Dave "Buster" Steward's family lived on the property. Club members got to keep their boards in the barn for free. Whenever out-of-town surfers would come to visit, they slept in the barn and surfed with SCSC members. (Courtesy Fred Hunt archives.)

Lloyd Ragon is shown on the beach at Cowell's with his laminated 12-foot plank. The round nose of the board was sheared off after a wipeout at Steamer Lane. It is widely thought that Lloyd was the first person to surf at Steamer Lane, as well as the one known for riding the biggest waves of the era (12 to 15 feet) at the Lane. (Courtesy Lloyd Ragon collection.)

From left to right, Claude "Duke" Horan, Harold Goody, Blake Turner, Harry Mayo, and Roy Melin ham it up in front of the "board house," the board storage area the SCSC was able to finally acquire just behind the pier bathhouse in 1940. Instead of carrying their heavy boards a block to the beach from the barn, the surfers now had much easier access to the waves. (Courtesy Fred Hunt archives.)

This rare water shot depicts Lloyd Ragon as he prepares to set a hard line toward the inside section at Steamer Lane on his 12-foot solid redwood plank. Ragon often rode the Lane completely alone during the late 1930s and early 1940s. (Courtesy Lloyd Ragon collection.)

On New Year's Day in 1944, members of the SCSC celebrate in front of their clubhouse, formerly a hamburger stand, with other members now in uniform. The club members finally had a place of their own right on the beach. The SCSC acquired the structure for $250 and used it until 1952, when it was unfortunately vandalized and set aflame. The City of Santa Cruz acquired the clubhouse from the SCSC and had it moved. It was the end of a classic era. (Courtesy Santa Cruz Seaside Company.)

Rich Thompson (left) and Harry Murray end a long tandem ride between the broken pilings and the main Santa Cruz Wharf. The two rode the wave from Outside Cowell's (Cypress Point) all the way to the beach on a 12-foot hollow board during a large south swell in the summer of 1941. After completing the ride, they then walked a few yards up the sand and stored the board away in the board house. (Courtesy Harry Mayo.)

Pictured is Harry Mayo's official SCSC membership card. It reads, "Santa Cruz Surfing Club. This is to certify that H. J. Mayo is a member in good standing and is entitled to all rights and privileges of this club. No. 11, June 1, 1946." It is signed by Harry Mayo and club president Richie Thompson. Southern California surfing legend Hoppy Schwartz's picture is featured on the card. (Courtesy Harry Mayo.)

The 1940 lifeguard crew included two SCSC members, Don "Bosco" Patterson and Lloyd Ragon. Pictured from left to right are Malio Stagnaro, Joe Hans, Les Eisley, Ernie Kiff, chief of police Skip Littlefield (kneeling), Delbert Colcough, Don "Bosco" Patterson, Don McNair, Lloyd Ragon, and Al Huntsman. The Santa Cruz Municipal Lifesaving Corps watched over the beaches and also the giant indoor swimming pool, the Plunge, located off Main Beach on the boardwalk. (Courtesy Kim W. Stoner archives.)

From left to right, Bosco Patterson, Jack Moore, Buster Steward, and Harry Murray share a long ride from Cypress Point to the beach. Cypress Point is the area members of the SCSC now call Outside Cowell's. Notice the cypress trees in the background; it is a much more fitting name for the break. (Courtesy Lloyd Ragon collection.)

18

Skip Littlefield, Director of the Water Carnival and Retired Pacific Coast Swimming Champion

PLUNGE CARNIVALS

The Man on the Flying Trapeze. Don Patterson Extends Greetings to Willie Apple.—Stubby Kill

8:30 EVERY SAT. NIGHT 8:30

Positively the Most Thrilling and Sensational of all

AQUATIC SHOWS

Fea- "THE 175ft. SLIDE FOR LIFE"
turing

MOST AMAZING FEAT EVER ATTEMPTED INDOORS

The "MAN ON THE FLYING TRAPEZE"

—BACK TO THE DAYS OF BARNUM & BAILEY—

RUTH KAHL
The Human Submarine
Greatest Underwater Swimmer Of All Time

DON PATTERSON
Supreme in Comedy, Thrills, Aerial Sensations, Performer of the Death Defying Fire Dive

DEATH DEFYING FIRE DIVE

"GREATEST OF ALL AQUATIC THRILLS"

THE HUMAN

SUBMARINES

ENDURANCE BEYOND BELIEF

WILLIE APPLE

Champion Swimmer of Tasmania

$10,000 Challenge to any Swimmer in the World who can Defeat this Strange Character

10 GREAT EVENTS

Champion Swimmers and Divers in Action. ◻Side Splitting Comedy Antics ◻Breath Taking Feats ◻The Show of Shows

PLUNGE WATER CARNIVALS

Santa Cruz Natatorium at the Beach, "Where Everybody Goes on Saturday Night"

SCSC member and daredevil Bosco Patterson was featured in the famous Plunge Carnivals of the 1940s. He was most famous for his daring "slide for life" routine. He would suspend from a cable tied to the top of the casino before sliding down across the beach with a partner hanging from his legs. Then, as the duo approached the Pleasure Pier, he would jump into the ocean, barely missing the pilings. Another favorite from the era was his famous "fire dive," which was billed as the "greatest of all thrills." At night, he would slide down the cable completely on fire before disappearing in the dark ocean. As the center of these carnivals, the Plunge pumped in saltwater from the bay across Main Beach and added fresh water at a 50/50 ratio. During huge surf periods with high tides, waves would sometimes wash away the beach, flood the boardwalk, and inundate the pool. Some members of the SCSC worked at the Plunge as lifeguards during the summer months. (Courtesy Kim W. Stoner archives.)

Next to the clubhouse and just back from a trip to Pleasure Point are (from left to right) Rich Thompson, Duke Horan, Harry Mayo, and E. J. Osher. It was Horan who named Steamer Lane one day at Cowell's. He looked out at the huge breakers and said, "My God, they're breaking out in the steamer lanes," referring to the routes ships would take up and down the coast delivering redwood. (Courtesy Fred Hunt archives.)

SCSC members are huddled up next to the shale cliff at Cowell's for a beach party on a cool fall day in 1941. Joining the club members are Jane Fairchild, Pat Collins, Shirley Templeman, and Marian Franklin. Even on chilly afternoons without any surf, there was nothing quite as nice as hanging out on the beach with friends. (Courtesy Fred Hunt archives.)

The board house was much appreciated by the members of the SCSC. Instead of having to lug their huge boards from the barn, up Bay Street and a block away, they were able to store them a few yards from Cowell's Beach. The board house was located directly behind the bathhouse next to the main wharf. Shown here are a variety of the styles of surfboards used by the club during those early years. (Courtesy Fred Hunt archives.)

Lee "Scorp" Evans shoots the section at Inside Cowell's in the mid-1930s on his finless, 14-foot hollow paddleboard. Evans got the plans for the board from *Popular Mechanics* magazine and built it in shop at Santa Cruz High School. After this board, he built a 10-foot hollow board with a fin. Lee recalls surfing Cowell's alone for many weeks at a time during those years. (Courtesy Lee Evans.)

The entire club poses here in 1941 with a few friends in front of the bathhouse by the wharf. Hot days on the beach were welcomed by SCSC members once they emerged from the chilly waters of the bay. (Courtesy Fred Hunt archives.)

From left to right, Alex Hokamp, E. J. Osher, Duke Horan, and Lee Sparrow clown around for the camera in the late summer of 1941. This photograph epitomizes the close camaraderie and fellowship that SCSC members were fortunate to experience. A few months later, Sparrow became a U.S. Marine Corps pilot with the outbreak of World War II, and many other members of the SCSC wore the uniform proudly. The war became the defining event that would change those innocent times forever. (Courtesy Fred Hunt archives.)

Two

SOUTH COUNTY

Southern Santa Cruz County, known as "the Beaches," offers miles of pristine sandbars. The Moana Makani Surf Club (MMSC), from Manresa State Beach, and the Rio Surfing Organization (RSO) have vied for territorial surfing honors since 1965 with their annual longboard surfing contest, the longest-running surfing event in the county. In this photograph, south county ripper Teac Gillette streaks across a hollow wall in classic style from the right, while a totally stoked Boots McGhee hoots in the foreground. (Photograph by Terry Smith.)

South county surfer and artist Rick Stiff has designed many of the posters for the annual MMSC versus RSO surfing contest. The event is always a hooter of an affair in and out of the surf. Both clubs have outstanding surfers who compete fiercely for top honors. The event, held during the summer, ends with a full-tilt barbeque party on the beach. (Courtesy Rick Stiff.)

Longtime "goofy foot" style master Ed James ducks down as a thick lip descends on a glassy overhead tube at a south county secret spot. For more than 50 years, James has been a mainstream fixture in Santa Cruz culture. Always surfing without the aid of booties, even on the coldest of days, James prefers the barefoot feel on the deck of his board. (Photograph by Boots McGhee.)

Pictured from left to right on a frigid fall day in 1966, "Rio Rats" Hunter Morris, Terry Smith, Keith Smith, Steve Hull, Mike Glass, Teac Gillette, and Rick Stiff congregate at Platforms on the beach at Rio Del Mar. Even though it is late in the season, they prefer wearing the more maneuverable vests over the thicker, more cumbersome full-length wet suit jackets. (Photograph by Wayne Hull.)

RSO and MMSC contestants sun out with cold brews during the annual surf event. Included in this shot are Mike Wilson, Kurt Stevens, Paul Rigger, Brett Enders, Clarence Prado, John Cornett, Drew Johnson, and Jay Welty. The two surf tribes from the Beaches always have a great time together, sharing many a laugh and swilling many a beer during the contest. (Courtesy Mike Wilson.)

Both clubs pose for the camera at the beginning of a long day on the beach. The annual gathering brings out all of the south county's surfing elite and their families for a fun day in the sun, capped off with a huge barbeque and party. The weather is usually hot once the "pea soup" fog burns off and water temperatures, as they do in the summer, rise up to near 70 degrees Fahrenheit. The shallow, sandy bottom reflects the suns rays back up to the surface unlike other areas of Santa Cruz County, creating warmer conditions. Because the wide exposed beaches in the south county have nothing to block the wind, the surf can be blown out easily. But when it is smooth and glassy, the Beaches can produce incredible sandbar tubes with only a few surfers in the water. (Courtesy Terry Smith archives.)

Pictured is a Rio Surfing Organization (RSO) club patch. RSO was formed in 1965 by some Rio Del Mar members of the older Moana Makani Surf Club, which was formed in 1962, and was based out of La Selva Beach. They decided to start up their up their own group that would represent the Rio Del Mar area. With members sometimes called "Rio Rats," the group boasts some of the hottest surfers in the south county. (Courtesy Santa Cruz Surfing Museum.)

South county surf phenomenon Doug "Zach" Zacharias shows the classic soulful style that has won him top honors at the annual contest. In this shot, Zacharias is buried deep in an overhead tube. The Beaches can handle decent-sized waves when conditions are optimum. Outside sandbars can form up to 50 yards off the beach, creating long, steep tubular sections like this one. (Photograph by Boots McGhee.)

From left to right, Boots McGhee, Dana Saldavia, and Teac Gillette pose in the Santa Cruz Longboard Union's (SCLU) entry, "the mobile clubhouse," in the World's Shortest Parade held every year on the Fourth of July in Aptos. This makeshift float atop McGhee's 1945 Chevy pickup is loaded with classic longboards from the era. Represented are boards by Wardy, Hansen, Yount, Johnny Rice, O'Neill, Doug Haut, and Hobie. The parade runs down one block in downtown Aptos before veering off onto side streets. The SCLU was formed in 1982 to bring together the surviving members from all of the local 1960s surf clubs into one organization. The SCLU holds the annual Memorial Day Longboard Club Invitational Surfing Contest to raise money for local ocean-related charities like the Junior Lifeguards, the Surfrider Foundation, and the Santa Cruz Surfing Museum. It is the longest-running surf contest in modern times and attracts clubs from all over the state. (Courtesy Boots McGhee collection.)

The No Rules Contest is held sporadically at Manresa State Beach in the south county. Here members of the Upside Yer Head team, (from left to right) Pete Petersen, Bob Pearson, unidentified, Ed Guzman, and Vince Brolio, pose in full battle dress and are ready to rumble. Lying on the grass in front of them is their team emblem, a completely trashed surfboard. All boards displayed in the lineup were shaped by Bob Pearson, owner of Arrow Surfboards. (Photograph by Boots McGhee.)

Zane Astone (left) and Teac Gillette serve up some stiff cold ones from the Tiki Bar at the after-contest party of the MMSC/RSO event. The annual contest is actually more of a giant family fun day filled with laughter and camaraderie. Both clubs surf together on a regular basis, and most are close friends. As one participant put it, "Many a splendid time is had by all." (Courtesy Mike Wilson.)

Terry Smith perches on the tip of a super glassy wall at Sand Dollar Beach during the El Niño year of 1998. The warming ocean water event occurs rarely along the far south coast. The water temperatures are usually in the high 40s to low 50 degrees Fahrenheit along this stretch of the highway, and the onshore winds can blow frigid and hard. The rocky coastline and rugged shore are typical features of these environs. On this particular day, the air temperature was in the 80s and the water was in the mid-60s. Notice the one surfer without a wet suit. "Burger" Bob Shaw, Ed James, Rick Stiff, and Boots McGhee joined Smith on this surf safari to celebrate Rick's 40th birthday. For those willing to travel south of Santa Cruz into the desolate regions of the central coast, sometimes a treasure trove of empty waves can be found and shared by a small group of close friends. (Photograph by Boots McGhee.)

Sewer Peak at Pleasure Point goes off during the annual Log Jam surfing contest. Contestants must ride old longboards created before 1970 to be eligible to participate. The two-day event showcases boards not usually ridden for decades. Surfing legends of the 1950s and 1960s from up and down the coast congregate at Pleasure Point each year for some classic surfing on the heavy antique boards. No cords are allowed to be used. Most boards ridden in the contest range from 9 feet, 6 inches to 11 feet in length and weigh between 25 and 40 pounds. The low-tide reef at Sewer Peak is a difficult one to negotiate, with thick clumps of kelp and shallow rocks that jut out onto the surface. Pleasure Point usually breaks best at more medium-ranged tides. The contest always draws a large crowd of spectators as well. (Photograph by Dave Singletary.)

Three

PLEASURE POINT

Pleasure Point is located on Santa Cruz's east side. It consists of many well-formed reefs. Some of the most popular breaks are Sewer Peak, First Peak, Inside (Thirty-eighth Avenue), the Hook, and Sharks Cove. Betty Van Dyke is featured here on a balsa board surfing just off Thirty-eighth Avenue in 1954. (Courtesy Van Dyke archives.)

The Van Dyke family has been a Pleasure Point surfing dynasty from the earliest of times. Posing here on the porch of the Devines' Pastel Court cabin are, from left to right, (standing) Dave and Diane Devine and Tom Palmer; (sitting) Gretchen and Peter Van Dyke, Fred and Diane Van Dyke, and Gene and Betty Van Dyke. (Courtesy Van Dyke archives.)

In 1953, sunning next to a cliff on the beach at Thirty-eighth Avenue during high tide are Betty, Fred, Gene, Peter, and Gretchen Van Dyke with Russ McClellan. Sabella "Bill" Van Dyke, the Van Dyke brothers' mom, is sitting in the back row. The brothers' wide balsa planks lean against the cliff. (Courtesy Van Dyke archives.)

Ted Pearson and Pat Curren were two board shapers from mid-1950s. In 1957, they built boards together. Here their truck is parked in front of Gene and Betty Van Dyke's house on Thirty-fourth Avenue. The passenger side door of the truck had Pearson's name first, and the driver's side door had Curren's name first. They actually shaped a few balsa boards right on the beach at Thirty-eighth Avenue. (Courtesy Van Dyke archives.)

Ted Pearson planes down the rails of a balsa board on saw horses in front of his house, while Pat Curren attaches a fin to a board on the porch. Drawknifes and hand planes were tools of the trade for shapers during that era. The boards were then glassed and finished off in the garages, kitchens, and front rooms of many houses in the Pleasure Point area. (Courtesy Van Dyke archives.)

Betty Van Dyke poses with her Dale Velzy Pig model on the bluff at Thirty-eighth Avenue in 1957. She had just finished riding empty waves at Inside Pleasure. She sports a wet suit jacket that Jack O'Neill bought her on a visit to Santa Cruz; wet suits were a rarity during those years. This was prior to the time when O'Neill opened the Surf Shop in Santa Cruz in 1959 and the business was just getting off the ground in San Francisco. Jack's brother Bill oversaw the wet suit manufacturing side of the operation. Van Dyke recalls being able to camp right on the cliff at Thirty-eighth Avenue. When Jack O'Neill and his family came to town, they all slept in sleeping bags on the cliff right above the beach and had campfires. (Courtesy Van Dyke archives.)

A popular spot for left-breaking waves just to the west of Pleasure Point is Little Wind and Sea. This photograph shows a group soaking up some major rays on a hot late-1950s afternoon. Only the most skilled surfers of the era could ride the wide balsa boards effectively on these challenging, fast-peeling waves. (Courtesy Van Dyke archives.)

Some of the most famous surfers from the mid- to late 1950s gather for a Saturday night barbeque in 1954. From left to right, Jim Fisher, Rod Lundquist, Dave Devine, Peter Cole, and Bob Kitesworth joke around in anticipation of good grub. Fisher, Lundquist, and Cole set high standards for big wave riding at Steamer Lane during this era. (Courtesy Van Dyke archives.)

During a late 1950s trip down to Rincon, just south of Santa Barbara, Santa Cruz big wave legend Rod Lundquist (shown here) scrawled a humorous epitaph about his surf buddy, Peter Van Dyke, on the seawall. It reads, "Be it known to all, I Peter Van Dyke am the most outstanding surfer in the Blue Pacific." (Courtesy Rod Lundquist.)

From left to right, Jerry Colfer, Spike Bullis, Johnny Rice, Al Palm, and Mike Winterburn enjoy a pleasant acoustic jam session in the summer of 1956 atop the bluff overlooking Thirty-eighth Avenue cove. Notice the huge redwood fin on the tail of the balsa board here. On waveless afternoons, there was nothing better to do than share a few cold brews with friends at the beach. (Courtesy Van Dyke archives.)

In 1960, Al Wiemers (left) and Jerry Colfer share a laugh before paddling out at Inside Pleasure. They both have new foam boards from the era. During 1958 and 1959, blown foam blanks came onto the surf scene. Everyone gave up their old balsa planks for the new lighter foam models, which had more refined shapes and weighed much less, for greater maneuverability in the surf. (Courtesy Van Dyke archives.)

Joel Woods power planes the rails of a new lightweight foam blank in the early 1960s. Woods was one of the early shapers who created boards at the O'Neill manufacturing shop on Forty-first Avenue. Mike Winterburn and Jim Foley were the first shapers hired by O'Neill when the shop opened in 1959. O'Neill also blew his own foam planks in a concrete mold on site. (Courtesy Joel Woods.)

Santa Cruz native and shaping legend Johnny Rice stands above Inside Pleasure with a Velzy balsa he received from Alan Gomes in Southern California in 1956. Rice shaped balsa boards at Mitchell Brothers Surfboards in Santa Cruz during this time. In 1954, Southern California shaping guru Dale Velzy apprenticed Rice in the art of wood plank construction, shaping, and hand tool maintenance. Rice would meet up with Velzy at his shop in Manhattan Beach after high school and on weekends. Rice is one of the most prolific shapers in California surfing history, creating custom surfboards for more than five decades. He has traveled the globe in search of epic waves and has sustained himself throughout his life by his shaping prowess. His custom boards are still in high demand throughout the Santa Cruz/Northern California area and elsewhere. (Courtesy Johnny Rice.)

Pictured is Don Snyder, a Santa Cruz surf master from the late 1950s and early 1960s, in perfect trim about to enter the tube at Sharks Cove. Sharks Cove is the southernmost reef in the Pleasure Point area. Snyder lived directly across the street from Inside Pleasure and always found empty waves to ride. This shot was taken in the fall of 1961. Snyder sports the long-sleeved, beaver-tailed wet suit jacket, which was the suit of choice during those years. (Courtesy author's collection.)

Jack O'Neill stands in front of his shop on Forty-first Avenue in 1962. This was the location were he had a showroom as well as a surfboard and wet suit manufacturing shop. Featured here is the logo that Northern California surfing great Jim Foley designed for O'Neill. It was not long after that the company name was changed from the Surf Shop to simply O'Neill's. This is the site of the present-day O'Neill, Inc., business offices. (Courtesy Dave and Kathy Sweet.)

The Hook is one of the most popular surfing areas in Pleasure Point. It is a fast-breaking, long, reeling-off wall with several challenging sections. This classic painting by Pleasure Point artist Jim Phillips captures the feeling of surfing the Hook in the earlier days. A woody station wagon awaits two surfers, who are climbing up the steep cliff. The Hook was the meeting place for the Santa Cruz Gremlin Society (SCGS), a small surf club formed in 1961. The SCGS was the first surfing club to form in Santa Cruz since the Santa Cruz Surfing Club of the late 1930s and 1940s. Members included Jim Phillips, the author, Tony Mikus, L. J. Harris, Ron and Dick Lindsay, Gene Echeveria, and Denny Cox. Climbing up and down the muddy cliff to access the waves was always challenging, especially during and after rainy periods. Many a surfer has fallen off the cliff there, and some have been seriously injured. The rocky reef and jagged shelf along the cove were other hazards to avoid. But for those lucky enough to catch a clean wave there, the Hook was pure ecstasy. (Courtesy Jim Phillips.)

On a hot summer day in 1966, West Wind Surf Club member Joe Ayer slices a smooth line across a glassy wall at the Hook on his 10 foot two inch Haut Team board. Ayer wears the typical baggy trunks of the era. Stylish surfing is what epitomized the sport in Santa Cruz and California in general. Ayer was a casual and stylish waterman." (Photograph by Dave Singletary.)

Because of its close proximity to East Cliff Drive, the Hook can also get crowded. Here Craig Money snakes Mike Harrow and Jim Byberg as Larry Holter paddles out. This shot also shows the rocky beachfront where many a lost board was seriously dinged up. Surfboard ding repair was a thriving business during these cordless years. (Photograph by Dave Singletary.)

Early Pleasure Point pioneer Rich Novak tucks tight in the curl on his 8-foot short board. During an era of 9-foot, 6-inch to 10-foot boards, an 8-foot board was an anomaly. Novak would get blanks from O'Neill's, cut them down the center, glue in a 3-inch balsa stringer, and then shape them into smaller sizes. (Photograph by Bob Richardson.)

Joe Ayer drops down the face of a fast-peeling Hook wave "hanging five" while Geoff McCormick wades to shore. The heavier longboards of the 1960s made for great nose-riding vehicles once surfers had them in perfect trim. The added weight helped them plane through the water, creating stability and speed." (Photograph by Dave Singletary.)

The author is pictured here in front of the Pleasure Point Surf Shop in the fall of 1966 wearing his O'Neill surf team jacket. The shop was operated by Jeff "the Owl" White and Brian Bradley, originally from the Santa Barbara area. White had opened the Owl Shop across the street from Cowell's Beach in 1963 but wanted to expand business into the Pleasure Point area. The Pleasure Point Surf Shop carried boards by Owl, Yater, and Weber Performers. Chic Van Selus, Dave Kerr, and Stan "Birdman" Veeth worked the counter. White was an accomplished surfer and also a world champion dory racer. He and his partner Paul Hodgert competed all over the world, winning titles everywhere they went. Jeff's Owl Surfboards were manufactured in Summerland and then brought north to Santa Cruz. After the shop closed down, White returned to Santa Barbara and opened the highly successful Surf N Wear chain. (Photograph by Bob Richardson.)

Below, members of the PPSA pose before a sign announcing a trip they took to Mexico on May 13, 1965. Pictured from left to right are Gene Hall, L. J. Harris, Jim Phillips, Tony Mikus, Dave Sultzer, Leo Gurnoe, Tom Keinolz, Rick Metzger, Keith Monroe, and Gary Venturini. The PPSC was the most successful Santa Cruz surf club in local competitions during the 1960s. The club won the 1966 Norcal Club Invitational against teams from Santa Barbara and Pedro Point. Many of the members went on to ride some of the biggest waves of the era in Hawai'i as well. A few were also featured in several full-length surf films. Surfing clubs from the mid-1960s were popular throughout Santa Cruz County, highlighting standout surfers from every area. (Both, courtesy Jim Phillips.)

Joel Woods ducks under the lip of a fast-breaking Sharks Cove barrel. Woods was a master of the parallel stance used by several "goofy footers" of the times. Goofy footers are surfers who stand with their right foot forward when sliding to the right on swells. Rather than have his back to the oncoming wave, Woods would stand parallel to the sections for better stability and visibility. (Photograph by Dave Singletary.)

Artist Jim Phillips penned this hilarious caricature of Pleasure Point surfer Dennis Conquest. It depicts the sense of humor and lightheartedness of the era. Phillips's artwork was highly regarded throughout the nation. He also created posters for shows at the famous Fillmore Auditorium. (Courtesy Jim Phillips.)

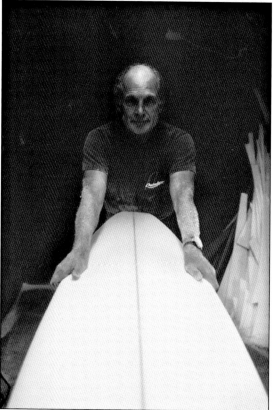

Doug Haut stands in front of his first shop in 1965 on Portola Drive in Pleasure Point. Haut shaped boards with George Olson before venturing out on his own. His reputation quickly grew, especially with the introduction of his famous Haut Signature series. Signature models had pulled-in noses with three stringers and thin rails for a real classic look with speed. (Courtesy Doug Haut.)

Shaper extraordinaire Doug Haut stands behind one of his foam creations in his shaping room on Delaware Avenue. He has continuously evolved his designs and templates from those early times into the present. His short boards of the 1970s and 1980s were highly sought after by discriminating surfers worldwide. His boards are some of the most popular wave-riding vehicles in Santa Cruz. (Courtesy Dave and Kathy Sweet.)

The West Wind Surf Club was formed in 1962. It was based in Capitola. Some of the members were Jerry Best, Ron Best, Dave Adams, Craig Throop, Vonnie Slater, Ken Edget, Jimmie Miller, Ken Phillips, Jimmie Dinsmore, Barry and Gary Hanby, the Machado brothers, Robbie Davidson, Rick Carleen, Joe Ayer, Joe Oster, Johnny McCombs and others. Below, East Cliff Surfing Alliance president Geoff McCormick cranks a hard bottom turn on a 1st peak left at the Hook. He rides a Phil Edwards tri-stringer. The East Cliff Surfing Alliance was also based out of the Pleasure Point area. McCormick later on became one of the presidents of the Santa Cruz Longboard Union. (Photogragh courtesy of Dave Singletary; above, courtesy of the Santa Cruz Surfing Museum.)

Gary and Jerry Benson worked in just about every surf shop in Santa Cruz during the 1960s, including O'Neill's, Olsen, Haut, and Scofield. They were both talented craftsmen who could shape, glass, and finish off boards to a very high degree. Their father, Ben Benson, designed this logo for them as a present; however, neither Jerry nor Gary ever liked it much and actually never used it. (Courtesy Dave and Kathy Sweet.)

Pictured in 1962 from left to right are Jim Phillips, George Olson, Jerry Benson, and Phil Lingman next to a "resin tree" created by stacking leftover colored resin containers used at Jack O'Neill's Forty-first Avenue shop. The fast-drying colored resin dripped down, creating a sculpture. (Photograph by Dave Puissengur.)

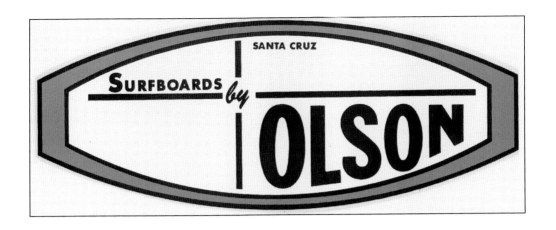

In 1964, George Olson left O'Neill's and opened his own surfboard company with Rich Novak. Olson did the shaping and Novak finished the boards off, doing tasks such as glassing, glossing, and polishing. Doug Haut honed his shaping skills at Olson's as well. Rich Novak (below) is cutting out a batch of fins from a laminated sheet of fiberglass with a ban saw. These were still the large block-style fins that briefly preceded the popular "shark fins." Olson surfboards quickly became popular at Pleasure Point surf breaks. The men continued their partnership until Olson decided to venture into the sailboat construction business, which became hugely successful for him. Novak and Haut went on to open Haut Surfboards in 1965. (Both, courtesy Rich Novak.)

Pictured here are Rich Novak (left) and Jimmie Phillips at Pleasure Point in the fall of 1963. The two men met years prior when one day Novak (one of the local "heavies" at the time) came down to the beach and yelled at Phillips and another surfer to get out of the water and never come back. Phillips didn't listen to him and later on, ironically, the two became the best of friends. (Courtesy Jim Phillips.)

Pleasure Point Surfing Association members Tom Kienholz (left) and Mark Angell opened their own surf shop in the early 1970s. Angell became one of the best foam craftsmen in town before traveling to the North Shore of Oah'u, where he shared a shaping room with the legendary Dick Brewer. Angell created his own templates based on the knowledge he learned from Brewer and quickly gained a reputation as one of the hottest upcoming shapers in Hawai'i. His boards were shipped to all the islands, and he gained greater stature as one of the best shapers in all of Hawai'i. Angell remained on the North Shore for a time, and then he moved to the island of Kauai, where he now resides. He continues to crank out a bevy of shapes for the residents there. (Courtesy Dave and Kathy Sweet.)

George Olson (holding daughter Christine) and Jimmie Phillips enjoy a couple of cold ones during a hot minus-tide day at Thirty-eighth Avenue cove. Notice that the reef at the Hook behind them in the distance is completely above the surface. With that low of a tide, the Hook becomes awash in thick kelp and is totally unfit for surfing. (Courtesy Jim Phillips.)

The 1965 Surf Fair, held in the Santa Cruz Auditorium, was a huge success. It featured surfboard displays, raffle prizes, surf films, and hourly prize drawings. The capstone of the event was the party/dance at night when all the different surf clubs joined in for a night of extreme merriment. A live band cranked out great dancing tunes, and everyone joined in with reckless abandon, hooting it up into the wee hours. (Courtesy Jim Phillips.)

FIRST ANNUAL NORTHERN CALIFORNIA

SURF FAIR

- PRIZE DRAWINGS EVERY HOUR
- DANCING
- MOVIES
- SURFBOARD SHOP DISPLAYS
- SURF CLUB DISPLAYS
- PLUS MANY OTHERS

Presented by the
PLEASURE POINT SURFING ASSOCIATION

SANTA CRUZ CIVIC AUDITORIUM

Donation **$1.50** ENABLING PATRONS TO LEAVE AND RETURN AT WILL

APRIL 15, 1965 • 10 A.M. – 12 MIDNITE
DURING EASTER VACATION

Four

THE RIVER MOUTH

The San Lorenzo River mouth is generally considered to be the demarcation line between the east side and west side of Santa Cruz. During heavily rain-drenched winters, a huge sandbar forms up from the runoff in the river. Surfers from both sides of town congregate there for intense surf sessions until the sandbar's demise in late spring. Here Ron Lindsay drives hard on the nose while Roger Dunham scans outside. (Photograph by Dave Singletary.)

The mid-1950s beach gangs loved hanging out at the river mouth in the summer. It was a great spot for both board and bodysurfing, strumming on a ukulele or nylon-stringed guitar, or simply sunning out with friends. Among those pictured here on a blazing June day in 1955 are Charlene Mohas, Peter McClean, Tom Burgess, Marge and Elaine Cranston, Betty (Mardesich) Van Dyke, Jose Angel, Jim Fisher, John Stoneham, Lloyd Kahn, and Dave McGuire. This was a great sandbar year. Bodysurfer Jim Houston recalled, "You could drop in outside the point and ride all the way past the pinnacle . . . that was considered a good ride." The waves peeled off both left and right, creating long lined brackish water tubes. And because the sandbar protruded out nearly 80 yards, it could be surfed during both high and low tides. (Courtesy Van Dyke archives.)

Dave McGuire charges right on his 11-foot balsa board in the summer of 1955. McGuire had to drive to Los Angeles to pick up the balsa for the board and then return to Santa Cruz, where Al Nelson shaped it. This was during the era of no wet suits. McGuire recalls, "Hey, you either surfed in the cold water or you didn't. That's all there was to it." (Photograph by Al Pease.)

Pleasure Point Surfing Association member Leo Gurnoe cranks a hard bottom turn on this steep river mouth barrel. The 1964–1965 sandbar was one of the best, and those lucky enough to ride it had nothing but smiles. The cold river water mixed with the ocean saltwater to create brown-colored tubes. A visiting Hawaiian surfer commented how the waves that year reminded him of island intensity. (Photograph by Dave Singletary.)

Tom Hoye races for the inside section during a high-tide session at the river mouth. Surf photographer and surfer Chic Van Selus paddles to the shoulder as Hoye bears down. Even though the water was sometimes only in the low 50s, many Northern California surfers preferred vests for greater movement. (Photograph by Dave Singletary.)

Santa Cruz Surfing Association member John "Johnny C" Craviotto seemingly glides on water without a board on a warm day in the summer of 1965. Even when the swell was small, the sandbar would pull in waves that could be surfed. Because of its massive bulk, the 1964–1965 bar lasted well into the summer. (Photograph by Chic Van Selus.)

Rich Novak, a 1950s Santa Cruz surfing pioneer, blasts through the takeoff bowl during the spring of 1965. Novak rides one his experimental 8-foot short boards here. He was a talented board maker who worked in all aspects of surfboard construction from shaping to finish. He went on to manage and own the successful NHS Industries. (Photograph by Bob Richardson.)

O'Neill team rider Jon Foster nose rides through the inner section of a wave in March of 1968. By the middle 1960s, most Santa Cruz surfers gave up their thin vests for the warmer long-sleeved wet suit jackets. Softer neoprene arrived on the market, enabling wet suit makers to construct warmer suits with greater flexibility. Foster remembers, "There was so much driftwood on the beach we had bonfires there all season." (Photograph by Tony Arkin.)

Jack O'neill and Jim Foley often times rode huge high tide waves during the winter at Steamer Lane on Jack's P-Cat. O'neill was not only a smart businessman but also a talented surfer and body surfer. who rode the Lane on the biggest days of the winter every year. HE and Foley would often times take off on huge waves at the Lane and ride them for over a quarter of a mile. Foley is also credited with the inventing the short board. During the 1960's longboard era, he was consistently designing and riding much shorter designs. He recently sailed a 40 foot sailboard around the world on a six year voyage. In this shot Mike O'neill and Robby Gong blast through the Rivermouth shore break in one of O'neills catamarans. (Courtesy O'neill archives.)

Five
COWELL'S BEACH

Santa Cruz's west side is home to some of the most demanding waves on the California coast. Steamer Lane has a world-renown reputation for its big grinding peaks, and Cowell's Beach is home to the county's cleanest fun surf. A long ride at Cowell's begins at a picturesque Cypress Point and ends up a 100 yards later at the municipal wharf. Here Jerry Colfer drives a hard bottom turn at Pier Surf in 1961. (Courtesy Santa Cruz Surfing Museum.)

The Van Dyke brothers and friends chill out in front of the Santa Cruz Surfing Club's clubhouse in the mid-1950s. Cowell's Beach was the main west side hangout spot in the 1950s and 1960s. With its close proximity to the waves, it was always a popular beach for sunning in between surf sessions. Out-of-town tourist girls always went there to sunbathe, which was another plus for local surf guys. (Courtesy Van Dyke archives.)

The Santa Cruz Beach lifeguards pose here in 1953. Assistant chief of police Don Lynn inspects the department lifeguard service. The lifeguards are (from left to right) Sam Reid, Bill Lidderdale, Gene Van Dyke, Al Weimers, Dave Devine, and Loren James. (Courtesy Kim W. Stoner archives.)

Below, Peter McClean (left) and Gus Gustavson pose with their balsa planks next to the shale cliff at Cowell's. Both of their boards were made locally at Mitchell Brothers Surfboards. These boards had the classic "chip" shape that was popular in the mid-1950s, which was also during the pre–wet suit years. (Both, courtesy Van Dyke archives.)

Ted Pearson (right) and Blake Turner celebrate a nice abalone harvest on the deck of the Santa Cruz Surfing Club clubhouse. The two men had just paddled in from harvesting the abalones from the minus-tide reef at Steamer Lane. They most likely tenderized the shellfish with a hammer then barbequed them right on the beach at Cowell's. (Courtesy Van Dyke archives.)

From left to right, longtime west side locals Mac Reed, Wes Reed, Al Fox, and Johnny Rice share a joke one hot summer day at the "office." After Fox retired from the County of Santa Cruz, he rarely missed a day sunning at Cowell's. He was down there so much he would tell people, "If you need me I'll be at the office," which meant under the beach umbrella. (Photograph by Rosemari Reimers-Rice.)

One the first surf shops to operate in Santa Cruz was the Mako Shop. Dirk Dirkson opened the shop in 1955. Mike Winterburn and George Olson were the shapers, and Rich Novak and Dennis Conquest finished the boards. Here artist Jim Phillips paints a romantic portrait of the shop. Much of the balsa that formed the cores for the 1950s boards came from discarded U.S. Navy life rafts. After World War II, the navy threw out literally thousands of balsa rafts, and clever shapers from the era stripped them down to carve out boards. However, General Veneer Manufacturing Company in Los Angeles offered beautiful straight-grained, 11-foot balsa strips for more discriminating shapers as well. The General Veneer stock could then be glued up with pine or first-growth redwood strips for a more beautiful plank. The navy rafts were often a mishmash of uneven and low-grade scraps, and were much more difficult to hone down. But, by 1958, balsa boards became extinct with the advent of the foam blank. (Courtesy Jim Phillips.)

Paddle races were popular in Santa Cruz during summers in the late 1950s and 1960s. Here contestants line up under the Ideal Restaurant awaiting the start of the 1959 race. Pictured are Don Piexoto, Dave Devine, Howie Spruitt, Danny Reed, Don Snyder, Dick Lindsay, the author, unidentified, Frankie Freitas, and Bill Laudner. Danny Reed won the race, with Don Snyder close behind. (Courtesy author's collection.)

This rare late-1950s shot shows Cowell's Beach at its best. Offshore winds, coupled with overhead waves and a dynamic sandbar, make Cowell's one of the finest right-hand point breaks on the California coast. Cowell's is a longboarder's dream come true, especially back in the late 1950s when the surf was relatively empty. (Courtesy author's collection.)

In 1959, Jack O'Neill opened up his first shop in Santa Cruz on Beach Hill next to Cowell's Beach. This was the first time local surfers could buy custom wet suits in town. The introduction of wet suits into the local surf culture was one of the most dramatic events in Santa Cruz surfing history. The added warmth made it possible to extend one's time in the freezing waters up to an hour or more, depending on the season. Surfing prowess entered a new dimension, especially in the difficult and challenging waves at Steamer Lane. Because the waves break so far off shore on big days at the Lane, the added warmth made it possible to stay out in conditions that were often bone chilling during frigid offshore wind days. The wet suit empowered surfers to take greater chances and push the sport into new realms of possibilities. A new era had dawned at the most challenging surf spot in the county. (Courtesy O'Neill archives.)

Gene Hall hangs five in the red-hot Cowell's shore break. In January 1961, the author waded into the freezing water to capture this action shot with his mother's Brownie Instamatic. This was one of the first photographs to be published in *Surfer* magazine from Santa Cruz. Hall went on to be one of the hottest surfers ever to emerge from town. (Photograph by the author.)

By the mid-1960s, Cowells began to see larger crowds as did other epic spots on the coast like Malibu and Rincon. In this shot Rod " the Bird" Tasic grabs a nice nose ride in front of another surfer in the white water. Notice the large block fin on the board in the foreground. THese types of fins were the standard fare before the advent for the sleeker "shark fins." The shark fins made turning a lot easier and didin't grab as much kelp. (Courtesy Dave Singletary.)

Otto and Jean Mayer operated the Fun Spot across the street from Cowell's. *Santa Cruz Sentinel* photographer Dan Coyro talked Otto into laying out all the boards he had collected for the classic shot seen above. Otto would pay surfers a small amount of money for their boards when they needed quick cash and thus amassed a huge collection. He also kept a monkey named Sam in a cage above the gas station. The business rented out surfboards, umbrellas, and surf mats to tourists. Notice the myriad shapes and styles of boards in his collection, a veritable 1960s surfing museum in its own right. Otto was a portly, colorful, outspoken character who was always looking for a deal. He could be seen on many a hot day napping on a makeshift bed in front of the station, as seen below. Local shaping legend Mark Angell cut his teeth as a shaper at Otto's Fun Spot in the early 1960s. (Above, photograph by Dan Coyro; below, courtesy Kim W. Stoner archives.)

In the spring of 1966, the Killer Cowell's Surfing Affiliation (KCSA) sponsored the Cowell's Beach Nose Riding Contest. The event was held on an epic 4-foot, minus-tide day and showcased the best talent in the county. Pictured in this crowd are Danny Anderson, Geoff McCormick, Tommy Ostrander, Bruce Phillipey, Mark Angell, George "Red-O" Arris, the author, Robbie Davidson, and Denny Taku. (Photograph by Dave Singletary.)

Winners of the Cowell's Beach Nose Riding Contest are pictured here from left to right: (first row) junior winners Mark Angell (first place), John Wargin (second place), and Mit Tasic (third place); (second row) men's division winners Danny Anderson (first place), the author and head judge, Rod Tasic (third place), and Roger Dunham (second place). Trophies were provided by the Killer Cowells Surfing Affiliation. (Photograph by Dave Singletary.)

KCSA and Scofield Surfboards team rider Alan Souza hangs heals during the Cowell's Beach Nose Riding Contest. Souza was one of the standout goofy footers from the 1960s. An avid west side surfer, Souza always pushed his surfing prowess into new realms and was a top competitor in contests. (Photograph by Dave Singletary.)

In the early 1960s, *Surfer* magazine held a contest to see how many surfers could be jammed into a car. In 1962, nineteen Santa Cruz surfers piled into Jimmie Phillips's 1951 Dodge across the street from the stairs at Cowells. This entry would have broken the record, but Phillips never sent it in to the magazine. (Photograph by Bob Biddle.)

Westside Longboard Coalition (WLC) member Kim Stoner gets a long five through the inside section at Cowell's, seen above. The WLC was formed to unite a small group of west side surfers from the 1960s. The club was formed in 1986, the same year a giant sandbar formed at Cowell's, which stretched halfway to the wharf. The club took that as a good omen. Members of the WLC shown below are, from left to right, (first row) Joe Grassi, the author, Chris Carey, and Kim Stoner; (second row) Jon Foster, Ed James, Gary Lamb, Alan Souza, Jay Collins, Ken Scofield, and Denny Moung. Larry Dunham was also voted in a short time later. The coalition held weekly barbeques and surf expression sessions on the sandbar until its demise in late summer. (Above, photograph by Phil Helsten; below, photograph by Kim W. Stoner.)

In the summer of 1966, the Santa Cruz Parks and Recreation Department sponsored a paddle race at Cowell's Beach. There were several divisions, teams, and individual races. Shown here is the beginning of the Unlimited Men's event, which meant there was no limit to the size or type of paddleboard an entrant could use. Gene Hall and Stu Fredericks check out the course that travels around the mile buoy before coming back to shore. (Photograph by Dave Singletary.)

This is a group shot of the winners in the paddle race at Cowell's Beach. Pictured in this group are Gene Hall, Keith Bridges, Doc Scott, Larry Holter, Robbie Davidson, Stu Fredericks, George "Red-O" Arris, Alan Behrendt, Jon Foster, the author, Louie Janosek, Marsha Carr, and Sue Hitchcock. (Photograph by Dave Singletary.)

The author jams a hard roundhouse bottom turn at Outside Cowells in the spring of 1965 on his 9-foot, 6-inch Yater Signature model board. The winter of 1964–1965 was an epic year for major sand movement along all west side beaches. The bar at Cowell's was so large and wide that during minus tides a person could walk out halfway to the wharf. The river mouth was also greatly impacted that year, which drew many surfers away from Cowell's. It was a lucky thing for devotees of Cowell's, like the author, as the usually heavy crowds had thinned out and opened up many overhead days like this one with few people in the water. The sandbars were so large that season they did not disappear until late in the summer. (Photograph by Dave Singletary.)

During the 1970s short board era, the author organized the Case of Beer Invitational Longboard Contest. Contestants had to provide a case of beer for an entry fee. The event was held on a low-tide day at the Cowell's sandbar in the spring of 1974. A deep hole was dug in the sand and all the cases were then thrown in. Contestants showed up with a variety of "old logs" kept stored away in garages. The winner of the contest was supposed to receive all the beer. The problem was there was no beer left after the final heat. The contestants seated (above), awaiting their heats, are (from right to left) Roger Rosner, Bill Killfoil, John Lusk, Chuck Reed, Chris Cole, Skip Hann, Larry Dunham, Hap Scott, and Ed James. Contest winner Chris "the Kink" Carey (below) smiles beery-eyed for the camera. (Photographs by the author.)

Rosemari Reimers and Johnny Rice were married on March 17, 1989, in the surf at Cowell's Beach, seen above. Many of their longtime friends joined them in the water for the actual ceremony. Rosemari was inducted into the Surfers Hall of Fame in Hermosa Beach in July 2007. She lived and surfed there as a young woman. The wedding ended with Johnny and Rosemari sharing a wave together. Johnny continues to shape custom boards for discriminating clients worldwide in his west side shaping room. Below, Rosemari glides on a wave toward the wharf after the ceremony with wedding veil still in place. (Photographs by Dean Nota and the author.)

Six

STEAMER LANE

Steamer Lane on Santa Cruz's west side is the most demanding surfing area in the city. With annual swells topping 15 feet, it remains the ultimate challenge for local surfers. First surfed in the early 1940s by Lloyd Ragon, it has a world-renown reputation. Here Don Piexoto drops into a steep face in the spring of 1964. (Photograph by Chic Van Selus.)

Big wave surfing legend Peter Cole was one of the mid-1950s balsa-era surfers to really open up Steamer Lane as a surfing destination. Cole went on to become one of the most famous big wave pioneers at Waimea Bay on Oah'u's North Shore. Cole is shown above streaking across a glassy wall in 1954. Many of the balsa boards that helped to pioneer the Lane were Hobie Makaha models, brought up north from Hobie's Dana Point shop. Cole poses below with two halves of his board after an unfortunate wipeout. This board was one constructed from a navy life raft (notice the irregular chunks of wood that make up the board's core). (Both, courtesy Van Dyke archives.)

Al Weimers was another big name at Steamer Lane in the mid- to late 1950s. His aggressive attitude in the surf paid off huge dividends on the biggest days at Middle Peak. He would often time ride the Lane alone during massive swell periods. Weimers went on to help pioneer surfing on the North Shore of Oah'u with other Santa Cruz surfers Peter Cole and Rod Lundquist. (Courtesy Van Dyke archives.)

Ted Pearson is shown here in 1954 charging hard on a lined-up Steamer Lane slot wave. Pearson was one of the first balsa shapers in town. He was a one of the driving forces to forge out a reputation in huge surf during the wild big wave era of the 1950s. (Courtesy Van Dyke archives.)

Rod Lundquist rode more big days at Steamer Lane than anyone in history. He would often paddle out without a wet suit in howling offshore winds and take off on massive waves that would bring chills down the backs of those on the cliff watching him. He and his close friend Jim Fisher became a legendary duo in huge surf. They also pioneered many spots north of Santa Cruz, including the daunting left at Greyhound Rock. Lundquist also rode giant waves in Hawai'i as well. Hawaiian big wave legend Fred Van Dyke once commented about Lundquist, "He was the most fearless surfer I ever knew." Lundquist is shown above at the Lane and at Sunset Beach, Hawai'i, below in 1959. (Both, courtesy Rod Lundquist.)

Don Snyder (above) and Danny Reed (below) were another dynamic duo of the late 1950s and early 1960s. They are famous for pioneering many Santa Cruz and North Coast surf breaks, including Stockton Avenue, Four Mile, and Davenport Landing. The author recalls being on hand with Bill Laudner on the beach at Davenport Landing the first time it was surfed in 1958, watching Snyder and Reed ride the lefts there. The duo went on to become two of the top surfers in Santa Cruz during those years, along with local great Jim Foley. Snyder and Reed were both legendary paddle racers as well. Reed rode boards shaped by early foam master George Dolitttle, while Snyder preferred Yaters and later became the Northern California representative for Yater Surfboards. Pictured above is Snyder at the Lane, while Reed is shown below rail-grabbing at Four Mile. (Both, photographs by Bob Richardson, courtesy Don Snyder and the author.)

This early-1960s shot by photographer Bob Richardson is a tour-de-force portrait of Steamer Lane at the height of its power. Caught inside and paddling hard with hearts in their throats are Jim Phillips and L. J. Harris. Going over the lip, Don Snyder, Rod Lundquist, and Rich Novak scan the horizon in anticipation of the next behemoth in the set. This shot also shows the many different choices in wet suits that surfers wore at the time: L. J. goes native, Jim sports a vest,

and Don, Rod, and Rich have opted for the warmer long-sleeved, beaver-tailed models for extra warmth. A wipeout at the Lane meant a long swim in through bone-chilling water to retrieve a board. That is, if it was still in one piece. And many novice surfers, held underwater, never made it back to shore at all. (Photograph by Bob Richardson, courtesy Rich Novak.)

In between sets, Don Snyder tosses in his board and jumps off at the Blow Hole. When the tide was medium to high, the easiest way to access Middle Peak was from the Blow Hole. It saved the long paddle from Cowell's or Indicators, especially if the rip was strong, which it always was on huge days. (Photograph by Bob Richardson, courtesy Santa Cruz Surfing Museum.)

The author climbs in the Blow Hole to retrieve his candy-caned Yater stuck inside. The jagged jaws of the Blow Hole "ate" many a lost board during the early days. It was not uncommon for boards to splinter apart after just one wave smashed them into the Blow Hole. (Photograph by Bob Richardson, courtesy author's collection.)

84

As the sport of surfing gained in popularity during the early 1960s with the advent of the Beach Boys and Hollywood films, crowds descended into town and localism reared its head around the county. Here an irate local surfer put up a sign on the pinnacle at the Lane showing his or her dismay. (Courtesy Kim W. Stoner archives.)

Surfing contests sprouted up in the early 1960s that showcased the local talent. In this 1962 awards ceremony after the Court of the Seven Seas event at the Lane are (from left to right) Hal Flafthauer, Joey Pappas, George Olson, Dennis Conquest, Johnny McCombs, Satch Bassinger, Jerry Benson, Rich Novak, and Bob Isles. Jack O'Neill, who donated the T-shirts for the event, sponsored the contest. (Courtesy Rich Novak archives.)

By the mid-1960s, the contest scene was a full-blown phenomenon. Every shop in town sponsored hot team riders who would wear their colors and ride their boards. Steamer Lane was the preferred spot for the events. These 1965 contestants, Tom Hoye, Gene Hall, Gary Venturini, Tommy Ostrander, Davey Sultzer, and some "surf bunnies," check out Venturini's new Haut Signature model. (Photograph by Dan Noonan, courtesy Santa Cruz Surfing Museum.)

Dave Singletary, a 1960s surf photography master, checks the focus on his telephoto lens. Singletary was the most prolific shooter of the 1960s surf culture during contests at the Lane. He also shot advertisements for Jack O'Neill and was hired by *Surfer* magazine as a staff photographer. He was sent by *Surfer* to cover the 1967 world contest in Puerto Rico. (Courtesy Dave Singletary.)

It is standing room only for the huge crowd awaiting the final heat of the 1966 Norcal Championship at Steamer Lane. Contestants from as far south as Santa Barbara came to compete, as well as from San Francisco to the north. The event was held in overhead surf, giving the spectators, as well as the surfers in the water, a real thrill. (Courtesy Dave Singletary.)

Killer Cowells Surfing Affiliation member Chris "the Kink" Carey displays style and grace as he hangs five during the semifinal heat of the juniors division. Even though the water was cold, Carey opted to go without a wet suit for more freedom of movement. Notice the baggy trunks that defined the era. (Courtesy Dave Singletary.)

Pleasure Point Surfing Association and Greek team member Danny "Butch" Anderson cranks a hard bottom turn with his arms buried in the water. Anderson was always pushing his abilities into new realms of self-expression in the surf. He was regarded as one of the top goofy footers of the era. (Photograph by Larry Daniels.)

Two contestants stand up on their boards as they glide through the top of this nice overhead wall. This technique was quite common for driving over the tops of waves in the cold northern waters. Rather than lie down and roll through the chilly waves, most surfers opted to stay as dry as possible. (Photograph by Larry Daniels.)

For those surfers unfortunate enough to get caught inside at the Lane, it was a real test of strength and perseverance; there were few options. A person either had to "go turtle," roll over underwater with only the surfer's bottom taking the brunt of the wave's energy, or stay on top and sink the nose as the wave passed over. Either choice was grueling. (Photograph by Larry Daniels.)

A mat surfer braces for a hard landing at the bottom of a reeling Steamer Lane slot wave. Mat surfing was popular in the 1960s as an alternative to board surfing. Sometimes on huge high-tide Middle Peak days, the only takers in the water were mat surfers and bodysurfers. (Photograph by Larry Daniels.)

Pictured here are Pleasure Point Surfing Association members (from left to right) Keith Monroe, Tom Keinholz, Tom Hoye, and Joel Woods hobnobbing with Southern California surfing great, Dale Dobson. Dobson was one of the top surfers in all of California during the 1960s. He almost always placed in the top three spots and usually won most events he entered. Tom Hoye was the top-rated surfer in Northern California but rarely ventured south for contests. Most Northern California surfers preferred the less hectic surf scene in Santa Cruz to that of Los Angeles and the South Bay. Plus the waves in Santa Cruz were usually bigger and more challenging than those down south. Most Southern California surfers did not like the colder northern waters either, opting for the cleaner surf conditions and warmer waters in the southern part of the state. But it was always fun and interesting to meet up and surf with each other during competitions. (Courtesy Dave Singletary.)

Entrants in the women's division of the 1966 Norcal Championship lug their heavy boards down the cliff into the cove at the Lane. Notice the large fin and multi-stringer designs of the times. Even though the boards were glassed with two layers of 10-ounce fiberglass, the rocks at Steamer Lane could bust a board to pieces in no time. (Courtesy Dave Singletary.)

Santa Cruz women's surf champion Jane McKenzie drives hard under the lip of a fast-peeling Lane section. McKenzie has won more contests at the Lane than any woman in history. Her stylish and aggressive moves make her one of the best female surfers in all of California. (Photograph by Boots McGhee.)

O'Neill team rider Dave "D. A." Adams blasts through a tough section during a contest at Steamer Lane in 1965. He is riding an experimental speed design shaped by Jerry Benson. Jim Foley also cut a section out of the center of the fin to create a hollow foil. Experimental designs were always a part of the surfing industry in the 1960s. (Photograph by Mark "the Melon" Harkleroad.)

This interesting perspective of Haut team rider Gary Venturini was taken atop the cliff at Point Surf at Steamer Lane by photographer Larry Daniels in 1966. Venturini was one of the smoothest and most aggressive local surfers of the 1960s, and he was always on the cutting edge in terms of style and grace. (Photograph by Larry Daniels.)

Steve Scofield operated Scofield Surfboards in the mid-1960s. Phil Lingman was the head shaper, and Jerry Benson glassed and finished off the boards. Scofield team riders included Alan Souza, the author, Ron Lindsay, Alan Behrendt, Dave Adams, Denny Cox, and Randy Selby. (Courtesy Santa Cruz Surfing Museum.)

Steve Scofield presents trophies to finalists at the second-annual Northern California Surfing Championship. Pictured here is men's division winner Gary Venturini in polka-dotted baggies; third-place winner Ron Lindsay smiles behind him. Steve sponsored many surfing events during the late 1960s, including the Class A State Surfing Championship on November 26–27, 1966, and the third-annual Steve Scofield Open Surfing Championship in March 1967. (Photograph by Dave Singletary.)

"Rockin' Robbie" Davidson explodes from a hollow section while perched on the tip of a small Steamer Lane inside wave. Even on small days, the Lane offers quality surf, which is why most major contests in the county are held there. However, when the tide sucks out, the inside sections are lined with big kelp clumps and exposed rocks. (Photograph by Dave Singletary.)

As stated in the caption above, the kelp beds at Steamer Lane were notorious hazards during the cordless 1960s. This unidentified surfer found this fact out the hard way. The thick kelp clumps could stop a board in its tracks, ejecting the rider into precarious positions. (Photograph by Dave Singletary.)

Early-1960s surfer Tom Leonard is about to pay a hefty price at Middle Peak. The strong offshore winds, blowing up the face of the swells, tend to create steep takeoffs that sometimes hamper boards from dropping in early enough to avoid catastrophes. Imagine being pitched like this, on a freezing winter day without a wet suit, 80 yards from shore. No one but the brave need apply. This shot also illustrates the tremendous amount of power and energy that Steamer Lane waves are capable of unleashing. No wonder so many boards have been snapped in half out there. And the toll on the human body is incredible. The author remembers one nearly fatal day in the winter of 1960 when the waves were in the 15-foot range. An unlucky surfer lost his board and had to swim in through the rip all the way to Cowell's shore break. He crawled up onto the sand, throwing up blood. He was never seen in town or at the Lane again. (Photograph by Bob Richardson, courtesy Rich Novak.)

Pleasure Point Surfing Association and Greek team rider Danny Anderson "hangs ten" on a glassy inside wave at the Lane in 1966. This shot also illustrates how glassy the conditions can get at Inside Steamer Lane due to the kelp and cliffs. The kelp beds hold back the low-blowing onshore winds from "chopping out" the surface, and the cliffs act as natural wind-blocking features as well. (Photograph by Dave Singletary.)

The Keinolz brothers, Joe (left) and Tom, celebrate their victories during the awards ceremony at a 1960s contest at Steamer Lane. Both Joe and Tom were members of the Pleasure Point Surfing Association and were active in contests during that era. (Photograph by Dave Singletary.)

Jim Foley cuts a hard line down a steep Middle Peak face. Even in the smaller overhead size range, Steamer Lane waves pack a big punch. Notice how thick the lip is on this wave. Swells move in from the deeper bay waters, hit the rocky reef, and pitch over with a vengeance. Foley was always one of the most aggressive and stylish surfers to ride the Lane in the late 1950s and 1960s. He rode both small and large surf with great skill and poise. As one of the true pioneers in Northern California surf history, Foley was also an innovative board designer and craftsman. His early experiments with board sizes and shapes led to the initial development and inception of the short board era, which has dominated the surfing culture ever since. Foley was instrumental in helping Jack O'Neill launch his early-1960s manufacturing business in Santa Cruz and designed the O'Neill logo. (Photograph by Dave Singletary.)

Tom Hoye shows the graceful style that made him one of Santa Cruz's top surfers during the 1960s. Hoye was rated No. 1 in the Norcal Competition for the year 1966. He worked as a laminator at O'Neill's until friend Joel Woods introduced him to shaping. He eventually left O'Neill's to open his own business, Tom Hoye Surfboards, in the early 1970s. By the mid-1970s, Hoye moved to western Australia, where he continued to make boards and ride empty waves in the Yallingup area. Here he slams a deep bottom turn and sets his rail for the long-walled section of a Steamer Lane slot wave. Slot waves are swells that line up from Point Surf and reel off all the way into Middle Peak. If one timed it just right and were lucky enough to make the big bowl at Middle Peak, he or she could continue riding all the way into Indicators and outside Cowell's. (Photograph by Dave Singletary.)

In 1968, Killer Cowells Surfing Affiliation member Alan Behrendt shows a casual style and cool demeanor as he sets a long rail for the challenging wall at the slot. He is riding a 10-foot Doug Haut For Pleasure Only model. Haut designed the logo in 1967 and used it on his boards in 1968 and 1969. By 1969, the surfboard industry was switching to shorter designs. The 8-foot, 6-inch to 8-foot, 10-inch V-bottoms became popular designs, and then, by 1970, the short board revolution exploded onto the scene. (Courtesy Jon Foster.)

The author jams a roundhouse, drop-knee cutback at the Lane in 1966. He rides his 9-foot, 6-inch O'Neill Intruder model team board. The Intruder was one of O'Neill's most popular designs during those years. The O'Neill team boasted many of the top surfers in town. Tom Hoye, Joel Woods, Dick Keating, Dave Adams, and Jon Foster were all members. (Photograph by Dave Singletary.)

Mark Angell tears it up at the slot during the 1966 Norcal Championship. Angell was one of the most talented surfers of the 1960s Santa Cruz scene. He became one of Santa Cruz's finest shapers as well. After he opened Keinolz/Angell Surfboards with fellow Pleasure Point Surfing Association member Tom Keinolz, he moved to Hawai'i and began a decades-long career there, establishing himself among the most sought after designers in the islands. He lived on Oah'u's North Shore and shaped for Haleiwa Surfboards in the mid-1970s. His boards became so popular on the neighbor islands that he eventually moved to the north shore of Kauai, where he currently resides. He has also won the Pine Trees Longboard Surf Contest in Hanalei Bay. (Photograph by Dave Singletary.)

Santa Cruz surf legend Gary Venturini is buried deep inside this super hollow Stockton Avenue Barrel. Venturini was known for his smooth and aggressive approach to surfing on both small and large waves. This shot was featured in *Surfer* magazine in the mid-1960s. (Photograph by Bob Richardson, courtesy author's collection.)

Style master Gene Hall blasts through a mean Steamer Lane slot wave in 1965. The windy offshore conditions can create super hollow tubes fit for a king, which by the way is Hall's nickname. He was also one of the first surfers from Santa Cruz to appear in a color photograph in *Surfer* magazine in 1962. (Photograph by Chic Van Selus.)

Contest winners share the jovial mood after the awards ceremony of the 1966 Norcal Championship at Steamer Lane. Pictured among the crowd are Chris Carey, Alan Souza, Davey Seltzer, Gary Venturini, Rick Kalinoski, Mit Tasic, Jan Jedlica, and Dave Devine. The contest was sponsored by Johnny Rice Surfboards and Steve Scofield. (Photograph by Dave Singletary.)

Steamer Lane was always the preferred venue for holding surfing events in the 1960s. The many reef configurations could pull in a variety of swells from any direction, and the cliffs and boulders were perfect viewing spots for both spectators and photographers alike. It still remains one of the most challenging places to surf in the world. (Photograph by Dave Singletary.)

The Santa Cruz Surfing Association (SCSA) was the premiere Westside surf club in the mid-1960s. The club wore black nylon jackets with black and white patches. The SCSA membership contained most of the Westside greats from the era. The club was run by Steve Scofield (president), Bob Biddle (vice president), and Denny Moung (treasurer). Other members included Chic Van Selus, Don Piexoto, Ray Lee, Ray Dalbesio, John Craviotto, Jeff Locke, Dave Thomas, Meryl Craig, Bob Judd, Rick Huber, Tom Estrada, and John Wargin. The SCSA held meetings throughout the Westside and kept their boards at Bob Biddle's house, half a block from the stairs at Cowell's Beach. The capstone event for the club was the fiercely competitive contests they had against the West Wind Surf Club (WWSC) at Steamer Lane in 1965. A final tally concludes that the WWSC has won by a slim margin. The event was held in 6- to 8-foot surf and was one of the best events ever held at the Lane. (Courtesy Santa Cruz Surfing Museum.)

Sam Reid (left) and Gene Van Dyke are shown here at Cowell's in 1954. Both men were lifeguards and surfers. A wooden sign was erected next to stairs at Cowell's to honor Sam's Traditional Rules of Surfing, "1) Paddle around wave, not through it 2) First surfer on wave has right-of-way 3) Hang on to your board, and 4) Help fellow surfer." (Courtesy Van Dkye archives.)

Master shaper Johnny Rice carves the rails of a redwood board with a hand plane. Rice continues to make custom boards of all sizes, shapes, and materials for the discriminating customer. Few modern shapers even know how to build boards like this one. (Photograph by Rosemari Reimers-Rice.)

Many of the lifeguards of the 1950s and 1960s were surfers. This shot of the guards in 1954 shows (from left to right) Harry Jacobson, Tom Saunders, Rod Lundquist, Dave McGuire, White Cloud, and two others in top form. The boards on which they are sitting are 12-foot to 14-foot hollow paddleboards. To keep in shape, they had daily running, swimming, and paddling workouts. Rod Lundquist went on to become one of the most celebrated big wave surfers in the world. (Courtesy Santa Cruz Seaside Company.)

Four Mile Beach sits just north of Santa Cruz on Highway 1. It was first surfed in the late 1950s. At the time, a roadway down to the beach was open. After some errant surfers drove over and busted the farmer's irrigation pipes, he closed access to the beach by car. These two shots depict a dynamic view of the takeoff area out by the point. A wave comes in and blasts the cliff, indicating a set. Then a surfer takes off by the rocky cliff, turns, and begins a long right sliding wall. Four Mile Beach was also a popular party beach during those times, and revelers could camp out on the beach overnight. (Photographs by Dave Singletary.)

Santa Cruz surfer and Cowell's Beach fixture Al Fox poses next to the "area restricted" sign at Trestles surfing area in 1957. Trestles was located on a U.S. Marine base in Southern California. He and Don Snyder had to sneak in through low-lying bushes with their boards, past patrolling marines, to access the surf. Santa Cruz surfers were not used to the rigorous restrictions found in Southern California. Notice the foam board in the back of Snyder's 1956 Ford convertible. Bill Laudner's mom got a Styrofoam blank, glued in a stringer, shaped it, glassed it with epoxy resin, and then gave it to him as a present. This was in the balsa era, and Snyder was riding a 10-foot Doolittle balsa board that sticks out of the back of the car. Snyder and Fox made quite a few trips to Southern California during those years. (Photograph by Don Snyder.)

Jack O'Neill helps Chubby Mitchell up the firehose at Steamer Lane in 1959. Before the stairs were constructed for easier access to the cove, a firehose hung down the shale cliff. There was the one-man, two-man, and three-man method for moving boards up and down the cliff. O'Neill and Mitchell are using the two-man approach. (Courtesy Santa Cruz Surfing Museum.)

Gary Venturini pulls off a classic stretch five on a small day at the slot at Steamer Lane. He is riding a Doug Haut "bump" nose rider model. The bump-style boards were carved out on the deck above the first third of the nose area. The idea was that the boards would plane better when the rider was perched on the tip. (Photograph by Dave Singletary.)

One of the great things about living and surfing in the Santa Cruz area is the pristine environment. Unlike Southern California, with its bustling traffic, mega-urban crowds, and smoggy air, Northern Californians believe their area offers a more beautiful environment and tranquil beaches. Artist Jim Phillips's painting *Tree Surf* perfectly encompasses this idea. Santa Cruz sits in the middle of the Monterey National Marine Sanctuary, which was set up to protect the fragile and diverse ecosystem here. Dolphins, whales, otters, and elephant seals all inhabit the waters surrounding Santa Cruz County. The local surfing community supports the preservation of this wonderful environment. Groups such as the Surfrider Foundation and the Santa Cruz Longboard Union take great pains to help preserve the natural beauty of the area. They provide annual fund-raisers to support those efforts. (Courtesy Jim Phillips.)

From left to right, Jay Shuirman and Betty and Gene Van Dyke hang out with Doug Haut in front of his first shop in the spring of 1966. Haut shaped with George Olson prior to opening his own place. He became one of Santa Cruz's elite board makers from then on. He was most famous for his three-stringer Signature models and his step-deck nose riders in the mid-1960s. (Courtesy Doug Haut.)

Doug Haut cranks a smooth bottom turn on a fast breaking left at the Hook in 1965. Haut was always known for his casual surf style even in huge surf. Here he rides one of his new 9-foot, 6-inch step-deck nose riders. He was a member of the Pleasure Point Surfing Association and has always been a major force in the Santa Cruz surfing community. (Photograph by Dave Singletary.)

Santa Cruz Surfing Association member Denny "the Fish" Moung drags an arm inside this hollow Stockton Avenue tube in the spring of 1965. Moung's stylish surfing demeanor was highly praised by many in the 1960s. The Westside Longboard Coalition used this shot as its club logo years later. (Photograph by Chic Van Selus.)

Santa Cruz Surfing Association goofy-foot ripper Ray Lee shows poise as he crouches on the tip of this river mouth on a left break in 1964. The 1960s era was one of stylish surfing in Santa Cruz. It sometimes seemed more like an art form than a sport, with the best surfers of the day striking casual, unique poses on waves. (Photograph by Chic Van Selus.)

Ed James throws a casual drop-knee cutback at a south county secret spot. The southern part of Santa Cruz County offers many spots that are not easily accessible, but for those who take the time to get there, a treasure trove of surf can be found. (Photograph by Boots McGhee.)

The bluff overlooking Thirty-eighth Avenue is the place where all Pleasure Point surfers hung out in the mid-1950s. The tradition has been carried forward by all other Point surfers ever since. Getting together with friends by the beach is commonplace throughout all of Santa Cruz County, especially in the surfing culture. There is no better way to create close friendships and lasting memories, which is one reason why the Santa Cruz surfing community is such a close-knit group. Pictured here at Thirty-eighth Avenue are Dave and Virginia McGuire, Gene and Betty Van Dyke, Tom Burgess, and Marge Cranston sharing a laugh with others on a warm afternoon in 1956. (Courtesy Van Dyke archives.)

Jack O'Neill's name is synonymous with surfing in Santa Cruz. Few people have locally influenced the sport more than Jack. Ever since he helped introduce the wet suit into the surfing culture here, the sport has blossomed in tremendous ways. Before then, surfing in Santa Cruz was limited in terms of how long someone could to stay out in the freezing conditions, especially in winter. O'Neill's wet suits turned all of that around. Surfers were able to attack the surf with much more confidence and warmth. In this photograph, O'Neill has received an award at the Surfing Walk of Fame at Huntington Beach in 1998. O'Neill wet suits continue to allow a new cadre of hot surfers to push the sport to higher levels in the frigid waters off Santa Cruz. O'Neill, Inc., is now a major player in wet suit development worldwide, and it also sponsors the O'Neill Cold Water Classic, a professional surfing contest held annually at Steamer Lane. (Courtesy Santa Cruz Surfing Museum.)

Doug Haut (left) and Davey Sultzer look over new board orders at the Santa Cruz Surf Fair in 1965. Every surf shop in town had a booth and got to show off their latest board designs. Members of the public also were able to meet and talk to team riders and swap surf stories. (Courtesy Dave Singletary.)

Pictured here are Tony Mikus (left) and Chris "the Turtle" Turrell goofing off in front of the original Dead Cow leather shop in 1971. Mikus is one of the finest surfboard laminators in Santa Cruz. He was a member of the Pleasure Point Surfing Association and has worked in many local surfboard manufacturing shops all of his life. (Courtesy Dave and Kathy Sweet.)

WELCOME TO

SATURDAY and SUNDAY JULY 16-17

SATURDAY and SUNDAY JULY 16-17

SANTA CRUZ BEACH

The Sensational All-Star Hawaiian Swimming Team, With

DUKE KAHANAMOKU

3 Times---World's and Olympic Games Swimming Champion---3 Times

CHAMPION OF ALL CHAMPIONS

Witness in Action
The
Greatest Swimmer
of All Time
THE MIGHTY
HAWAIIAN NATATOR
Who Revolutionized & Astounded the Aquatic World for Twenty-five Years.

Watch the Celebrated Swimmers from the Beach at Waikiki in Assaults on World Records.

Duke P. Kahanamoku, of Honolulu

Grand Exhibition
At
PLUNGE WATER CARNIVAL
POSITIVELY the GREATEST Aquatic Show ever Staged on Pacific Coast.

☞ RESERVED SEAT SALE now going on at PLUNGE OFFICE.

Combined Show with Santa Cruz Plunge's Nationally Famous Stars
IN THE GREATEST
WATER CARNIVAL
EVER PRESENTED with

RUTH KAHL "THE HUMAN SUBMARINE."
BOSCO PATTERSON "Man on the Flying Trapeze"
"Wild Bill" HICKOK, the amazing "Slide for Life"

WILLIE APPLE, of Tasmania. Watch him challenge Duke Kahanamoku. The Spectacle Magnificent "Death Defying Fire Dive" MAURICE KEALOHA and His HAWAIIAN ORCHESTRA and 10 other AQUATIC THRILLERS.

SANTA CRUZ PLUNGE & NATATORIUM AT THE BEACH

Hawaiian surfing great Duke Kahanamoku came to Santa Cruz to compete in a swim meet at the Plunge on the boardwalk in 1938. Santa Cruz Surfing Club member Don "Boscoe" Paterson also took part in the aquatic event by staging his famous "flying trapeze" act and also setting himself aflame during the "death defying fire dive" routine. The Duke was one of the famous Kahanamoku brothers who ruled the surf at Waikiki in the 1920s. Local surfing legend Sam Reid quit his studies at Stanford to move to Waikiki, befriended the Kahanamokus, learned the Hawaiian language, and became a well-respected surfer by the Hawaiians. He also won the Hawaiian Surfing Championship in 1928 and 1932. The connection between Santa Cruz and Hawaii has been strong ever since. (Courtesy Kim W. Stoner archives.)

Santa Cruz standout Tom Hoye is pictured bracing for the hollow lip that is about to pour over him at Stockton Avenue in 1966. Stockton Avenue is widely regarded as the spot with the most hollow waves on the west side. Swells pull in from deep water before exploding on the shallow reef. Even when "the Avenue" is small, many a board has been snapped in half there by the power of the waves. (Photograph by Larry Daniels.)

Phil "Stone Age" Snowden glides past Point Surf, setting up for the bowl at Steamer Lane in 1966. Snowden was one of a small cadre of big wave riders in the mid-1960s who would paddle out to the Lane on huge days no matter how large it broke. He got his nickname for usually riding boards he made himself that were not as finely crafted as shop boards. But that never held him back from confronting the largest waves on hairy days. (Photograph by Larry Daniels.)

A favorite watering hole for Santa Cruz surfers travelling south into Mexico was the infamous Hussongs Cantina in Ensenada, Baja California. Here, in 1963, Howie Spruitt, Marcy Spruitt, and Bob and Jeanie Chitworth toast with Don Snyder and Janice Parker. Snyder was recently discharged from the U.S. Army. This became a rite of passage for many surfers heading south of the border on surf trips. (Courtesy Don Snyder.)

Pictured here is a nice shot of the river mouth before Small Craft Harbor. Before the harbor was constructed, waves would form and line up all the way to the cliff at high tide. After the jetty was installed, the sand backed up and caused the inner cove to become a wide beach extending out to the point. (Courtesy Don Snyder.)

Dick Keating glides along a perfect Hook wall in the summer of 1966. Keating was one of the highest-regarded surfers of his time. He was as comfortable on small, glassy, lined-up waves like this one as he was charging huge Steamer Lane. He was legendary as a big wave rider who dropped down the faces of some of the largest waves ever to break at Steamer Lane. (Photograph by Larry Daniels.)

The rocky shoreline at Steamer Lane spelled the end for many lost surfboards. This mid-1950s shot illustrates how the power of waves and a cliff can be a bad combination for a balsa board. Sometimes just the force of a big Middle Peak wave pounding down on a board could cause it to snap. (Courtesy Van Dyke archives.)

Rio Surf Organization member Rick Stiff has designed most of the posters for the annual Moana Makani Surf Club/Rio Surf Organization Invitational Longboard Surf Contest. The event brings the two clubs together for a day of surfing and frolic. The best surfers in the south county vie for bragging rights until the next contest the following year. (Courtesy Rick Stiff.)

South county ripper Mike Astone shows a casual style as he hangs ten at Platforms in Rio Del Mar. Astone wears the necessary full-length wet suit and hood for winter surfing in the south county. Even though the water is numbingly cold, he prefers to go without booties for greater feel on the deck of his board. (Photograph by Boots McGhee.)

Marty "Marty Mechanic" Schreiber checks out the surf at Pleasure Point in unique style. Using his surf carrier for a sunroof, as well as for transporting his board, Schreiber is well ahead of the pack. He has been a Pleasure Point fixture for several decades. (Courtesy Boots McGhee.)

Three surfers prepare to scratch over a breaking wave at Steamer Lane: to the above right, this surfer stands up to avoid being hit in the chest by the lip; to the left center is a man pumping hard for the shoulder; and the unfortunate soul in the foreground has to deal with the force of the wave breaking on him, which is not an enviable position to be in. (Courtesy Larry Daniels.)

Two of Santa Cruz's longtime native sons and surfboard designers Bill Grace (below) and Johnny Rice (right) pose with boards from different eras. Rice's laminated plank was constructed from wood procured from General Veneer in Los Angeles in 1948. Grace's new hollow see-through design was constructed by him in Santa Cruz recently. Grace was a member of the original Santa Cruz Surfing Club in 1936. He built some of the early planks for club members back then and continued to make boards into modern times, a span of more than seven decades. Rice began shaping in the early 1950s and was trained by Southern California shaping legend Dale Velzy. He is knowledgeable in both wood and foam board construction. At 84 years young, with 62 years of shaping experience under his belt, Grace may very well be the most experienced board maker in California. Both plan to carry on the timeless traditions of surfboard design and construction into the unforeseeable future in Santa Cruz. (Right, courtesy Jim Phillips; below, photograph by Boots McGhee.)

The history of women's involvement in Santa Cruz surfing harkens back to the earliest of times. Santa Cruz resident Dorothy Becker surfed with the Kahanamoku brothers in Hawai'i back in the early 1900s. She may well have been the first Santa Cruz resident to travel to and surf in Hawai'i. Therefore, it could be said that Santa Cruz women have played an important role in developing the sport locally and throughout the world. Since the 1930s, 1940s, and 1950s, women have always contributed greatly to the local scene. The matriarchs of the local surf culture pictured here are (from left to right) Earlene Colfer, Betty Van Dyke, and Rosemari Reimers-Rice, posing with others at the Women On Waves (WOW) Contest, which is held annually at Capitola. The WOW Contest brings together surfers from all parts of California to compete and share many fun times together. Other local standouts are Jane McKenzie, Brenda Scott-Rodgers, and Cathy Mayerhofer. The long tradition and influence that women have brought to the sport of surfing will surely prevail long into the future. (Courtesy Santa Cruz Surfing Museum.)

Surfers in Santa Cruz County have always been active in efforts to preserve the pristine beauty of the area. In 1972, a developer wanted to buy the land at Lighthouse Field, next to Steamer Lane, and construct a large hotel complex with two 22-story towers and a shopping mall. The surfing community fought back with fund-raisers and put together money to help defray legal expenses incurred combating the development. Some surfers even chained themselves to ancient cypress trees on the site. John Scott sold his car and took out a full-page advertisement in the local newspaper. The project was abandoned when the developer saw the tremendous public outcry against it. Local surfer and artist Jim Phillips drew up this great poster to help mobilize the troops. The benefit raised thousand of dollars for the legal defense fund. And in the end the surfers prevailed. Steamer Lane is still completely accessible to anyone who wants to enjoy the waves there, and Lighthouse Field was never commercially developed in any way. (Courtesy Betty Van Dyke.)

This humorous painting, *Merc Woody*, by surf artist Jim Phillips captures the feeling of surfing in Santa Cruz throughout history. Three friends have the car packed up with boards as they head off to the beach in search of sun, fun, surf, and camaraderie. They are so stoked to see epic waves reeling off that they drive right off the cliff. Since the earliest of times, this is what it has really been all about. It never really mattered what a person rode waves on: a mat, a surfboard, a canoe, a sailboat, or even using the human body to slide down the swells. It has always been an experience from the heart that maintains a deep respect for the natural surroundings. This is the greatest of things—the inner connection everyone can feel when all of these factors are in total sync. Surfing has always been a vehicle for entering into nature and the ocean and feeling the stoke of it all, and then going on to do it again and again. (Courtesy Jim Phillips.)

The Santa Cruz Surfing Club Preservation Society was formed in 2008 to oversee and gather funding for the ongoing survival of the Santa Cruz Surfing Museum. The museum is located inside the Mark Abbott Memorial Lighthouse, which sits atop the cliff overlooking Steamer Lane. In this photograph, some of the surviving members of the original Santa Cruz Surfing Club are symbolically passing the torch on to the new members of the club. Pictured from left to right are Johnny Rice, Rosemari Reimer-Rice, Dave Dyc, Kim Stoner, Bob Giles, Ward Smith, the author with the torch, Jon Foster, Pat Farley, Harry Mayo, Dan Young, Boots McGhee, Doug Thorne, and Bill Grace. Club member Boots McGhee was behind the lens for this shot. The ongoing mission of the club is to create public awareness about the long history of surfing in Santa Cruz and to raise money to defray the operating costs of the museum. (Photograph by Boots McGhee.)

The Santa Cruz Surfing Museum displays surfing artifacts and photographs from the long history of surfing in Santa Cruz (also known as "Surf City") and earlier times in Hawai'i. Surfers and surfing aficionados in the community have generously donated or loaned a great deal of inventory to the museum. Artifacts from the earliest times are on display, as well as more current memorabilia. The Santa Cruz Surfing Museum opened in 1986 and was the first of its kind on the U.S. mainland. Many people were instrumental in its formation and eventual opening. It remains an important fiber in the soul of the Santa Cruz community's identity. (Photographs by Boots McGhee.)

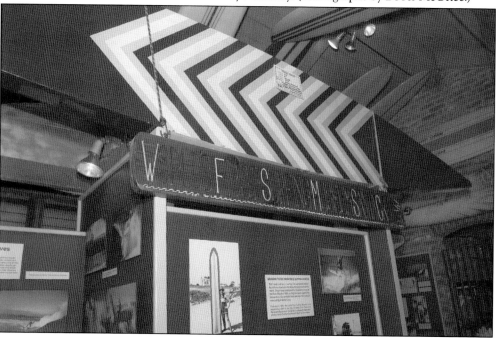

Surfing in Santa Cruz is a multifaceted experience. The community has some of the greatest surfers in the world as residents—professional surfers who are constantly seeking out ultimate honors and personal triumphs. It is also a community that supports even the most physically compromised individuals who would like to experience the personal stoke of riding a wave. The entirety of this consciousness is best described in a poem by one of the greatest California surfers of all time, Doc Ball, "When ol' King Neptune's raising Hell / And the breakers roll sky high / Let's drink to those who ride that stuff / And to the rest who are willing to try." The above image is of Dick Keating at Steamer Lane, and the image below is of Danny Cortazzo helping a young surfer feel the stoke. (Above, courtesy Dave Singletary; below, photograph by Boots McGhee.)

DISCOVER THOUSANDS OF LOCAL HISTORY BOOKS FEATURING MILLIONS OF VINTAGE IMAGES

Arcadia Publishing, the leading local history publisher in the United States, is committed to making history accessible and meaningful through publishing books that celebrate and preserve the heritage of America's people and places.

Find more books like this at
www.arcadiapublishing.com

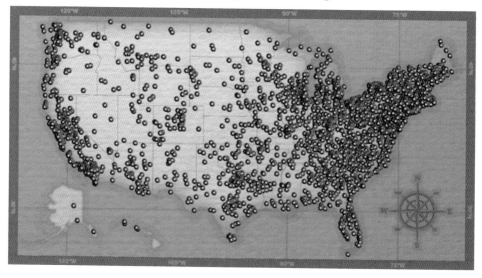

Search for your hometown history, your old stomping grounds, and even your favorite sports team.

Consistent with our mission to preserve history on a local level, this book was printed in South Carolina on American-made paper and manufactured entirely in the United States. Products carrying the accredited Forest Stewardship Council (FSC) label are printed on 100 percent FSC-certified paper.

MADE IN THE USA